♊ LOVE SIGNS ♊

GEMINI

May 22 – June 21

JULIA & DEREK PARKER

Dedicated to Martin Lethbridge

A DK PUBLISHING BOOK

Project Editor • Annabel Morgan
Art Editor • Anna Benjamin
Managing Editor • Francis Ritter
Managing Art Editor • Derek Coombes
DTP Designer • Cressida Joyce
Production Controller • Martin Croshaw
US Editor • Constance M. Robinson

ACKNOWLEDGMENTS

Photography: Steve Gorton: pp. 10, 13–15, 17–19, 46–49; Ian O'Leary: 16. *Additional photography by:* Colin Keates, David King, Monique Le Luhandre, David Murray, Tim Ridley, Clive Streeter, Harry Taylor, Matthew Ward. *Artworks:* Nic Demin: 34–45; Peter Lawman: *jacket,* 4, 12; Paul Redgrave: 24–33; Satwinder Sehmi: *glyphs;* Jane Thomson: *borders;* Rosemary Woods: 11.

Peter Lawman's paintings are exhibited by the Portal Gallery Ltd, London.

Picture credits: Bridgeman Art Library/Hermitage, St. Petersburg: 51; Robert Harding Picture Library: 20l, 20c, 20r; Images Colour Library: 9; The National Gallery, London: 11; Tony Stone Images: 21t, 21b; The Victoria and Albert Museum, London: 5; Zefa: 21c.

First American Edition, 1996
2 4 6 8 10 9 7 5 3 1

Published in the United States by
DK Publishing, Inc., 95 Madison Avenue, New York, New York 10016
Visit us on the World Wide Web at http://www.dk.com

A catalog record is available from the Library of Congress.

ISBN 0-7894-1091-5

Reproduced by Bright Arts, Hong Kong
Printed and bound by Imago, Hong Kong

CONTENTS

ASTROLOGY & YOU

THERE IS MUCH MORE TO ASTROLOGY THAN YOUR SUN SIGN.
A SIMPLE INVESTIGATION INTO THE POSITION OF THE OTHER
PLANETS AT THE MOMENT OF YOUR BIRTH WILL PROVIDE YOU
WITH FASCINATING INSIGHTS INTO YOUR PERSONALITY.

*Y*our birth sign, or Sun sign, is the sign of the zodiac that the Sun occupied at the moment of your birth. The majority of books on astrology concentrate only on explaining the relevance of the Sun signs. This is a simple form of astrology that can provide you with some interesting but rather general information about you and your personality. In this book, we take you a step further, and reveal how the planets Venus and Mars work in association with your Sun sign to influence your attitudes toward romance and sexuality.

In order to gain a detailed insight into your personality, a "natal" horoscope, or birth chart, is necessary. This details the position of all the planets in our solar system at the moment of your birth, not just the position of the Sun. Just as the Sun occupied one of the 12 zodiac signs when you were born, perhaps making you "a Geminian" or "a Sagittarian," so each of the other planets occupied a certain sign. Each planet governs a different area of your personality, and the planets Venus and Mars are responsible for your attitudes toward love and sex, respectively.

For example, if you are a Sun-sign Sagittarian, according to the attributes of the sign you should be a dynamic, freedom-loving character. However, if Venus occupied Libra when you were born, you may make a passive and clinging partner – qualities that are supposedly completely alien to Sagittarians.

A MAP OF THE CONSTELLATION

The 16th-century astronomer Copernicus first made the revolutionary suggestion that the planets orbit the Sun rather than Earth. In this 17th-century constellation chart, the Sun is shown at the center of the solar system.

The tables on pages 52–61 of this book will enable you to discover the positions of Mars and Venus at the moment of your birth. Once you have read this information, turn to pages 22–45. On these pages we explain how the influences of Venus and Mars interact with the characteristics of your Sun sign. This information will provide you with many illuminating insights into your personality, and explains how the planets have formed your attitudes toward love and sex.

LOOKING FOR A LOVER

ASTROLOGY CAN PROVIDE YOU WITH VALUABLE INFORMATION
ON HOW TO INITIATE AND MAINTAIN RELATIONSHIPS. IT CAN
ALSO TELL YOU HOW COMPATIBLE YOU ARE WITH YOUR LOVER,
AND HOW SUCCESSFUL YOUR RELATIONSHIP IS LIKELY TO BE.

*P*eople frequently use astrology to lead into a relationship, and "What sign are you?" is often used as a conversation opener. Some people simply introduce the subject as an opening gambit, while others place great importance on this question and its answer.

Astrology can affect the way you think and behave when you are in love. It can also provide you with fascinating information about your lovers and your relationships. Astrology cannot tell you who to fall in love with or who to avoid, but it can offer you some very helpful advice.

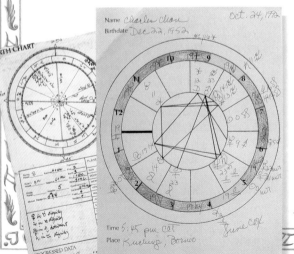

BIRTH CHARTS
Synastry involves the comparison of two people's charts in order to assess their compatibility in all areas of their relationship. The process can highlight any areas of common interest or potential conflict.

THE TABLE OF ELEMENTS

People whose signs are grouped under the same element tend to find it easy to fall into a happy relationship. The groupings are:

FIRE: *Aries, Leo, Sagittarius*
EARTH: *Taurus, Virgo, Capricorn*
AIR: *Gemini, Libra, Aquarius*
WATER: *Cancer, Scorpio, Pisces*

When you meet someone to whom you are attracted, astrology can provide you with a valuable insight into his or her personality. It may even reveal unattractive characteristics that your prospective partner is trying to conceal.

Astrologers are often asked to advise lovers involved in an ongoing relationship, or people who are contemplating a love affair. This important aspect of astrology is called synastry, and involves comparing the birth charts of the two people concerned. Each birth chart records the exact position of the planets at the moment and place of a person's birth.

By interpreting each chart separately, then comparing them, an astrologer can assess the compatibility of any two people, showing where problems may arise in their relationship, and where strong bonds will form.

One of the greatest astrological myths is that people of some signs are not compatible with people of certain other signs. This is completely untrue. Whatever your Sun sign, you can have a happy relationship with a person of any other sign.

YOU & YOUR LOVER

KNOWING ABOUT YOURSELF AND YOUR LOVER IS THE KEY TO
A HAPPY RELATIONSHIP. HERE WE REVEAL THE TRADITIONAL
ASSOCIATIONS OF GEMINI, YOUR COMPATIBILITY WITH ALL THE
SUN SIGNS, AND THE FLOWERS LINKED WITH EACH SIGN.

HAZEL TREES, AND
ALL TREES THAT
BEAR NUTS, ARE
GOVERNED
BY GEMINI

YELLOW HAS
THE CLOSEST
AFFINITY WITH
THIS SIGN

LILY-OF-THE-
VALLEY IS A
GEMINIAN
FLOWER

GEMINI IS RULED
BY MERCURY,
THE PLANET OF
COMMUNICATION

BUTTERFLIES ARE
TRADITIONALLY
ASSOCIATED
WITH GEMINI

TALKING BIRDS,
SUCH AS THE
PARROT, ARE ALL
LINKED WITH GEMINI

GEMINIANS TEND TO
BE TALL AND SLIM,
WITH A BOUNCY,
ENERGETIC STRIDE

GEMINI AND ARIES
Ariens and Geminians are both optimistic, lively, and entertaining. You have much in common, and this is a good combination. The depth and intensity of Arien passion may take you by surprise.

Lavender is a Geminian flower

Thistles are ruled by Aries

GEMINI AND GEMINI
You both enjoy discussion and debate, and there will be plenty to talk about when two chatty Geminians get together. You are both very flirtatious, and serious commitment will need care.

GEMINI AND TAURUS
Taureans take commitment very seriously; therefore, you should control your flirtatious behavior. If you can both overcome your considerable differences, your relationship can be very happy.

The lily, and other white flowers, are ruled by Cancer

The rose is associated with Taurus

GEMINI AND CANCER
You two have very different aims. Gemini wants excitement, while Cancer needs domestic security. If you can curb your restless streak, a Cancerian may trust you with his or her happiness.

GEMINI AND LEO

Leo represents dignity, while you are impudence. You may find Leos too pompous, and they may see you as frivolous. Overcome this mutual disapproval, and you will have a stimulating relationship.

Hydrangeas are governed by Libra

Sunflowers are ruled by Leo

GEMINI AND LIBRA

Geminian liveliness will boost Libran energy levels, and the placid Libran influence will calm your restlessness. However, you may not be able to provide the security that Libra is seeking.

GEMINI AND VIRGO

Both signs are ruled by Mercury, the planet of communication; therefore, you will have plenty to discuss. Virgos may not approve of your flightiness, but you are potentially a strong couple.

Honeysuckle is attributed to Scorpio

Small, brightly colored flowers are associated with Virgo

GEMINI AND SCORPIO

Geminians may find it difficult to realize the depth of Scorpio emotions. Your Scorpio lover will respond to any flirtatiousness on your part with a surprisingly powerful jealous rage.

GEMINI AND SAGITTARIUS
Both Geminians and Sagittarians are footloose novelty seekers, and you make a perfect match. Both of you are witty, gregarious, and entertaining, and will share a lively and carefree existence.

Orchids are associated with Aquarius

Carnations are ruled by Sagittarius

GEMINI AND AQUARIUS
Aquarian eccentricity will amuse you, and you will be attracted to the sociable side of the Aquarian personality. They take loyalty very seriously, and may not appreciate your flirtatiousness.

GEMINI AND CAPRICORN
Capricorns have a dry sense of humor, which you will appreciate. However, they take life seriously. You may be too flighty for them, although they will provide you with a stabilizing influence.

Viburnum is governed by Pisces

Pansies are Capricorn flowers

GEMINI AND PISCES
Pisceans are emotional and passionate partners, and your lighthearted approach to love may upset them. Emotional storms could be triggered by your flirtatiousness.

THE FOOD OF LOVE

WHEN PLANNING A SEDUCTION, THE SENSUOUS DELIGHTS OF AN
EXQUISITE MEAL SHOULD NEVER BE UNDERESTIMATED. READ ON
TO DISCOVER THE PERFECT MEAL FOR EACH OF THE SUN SIGNS,
GUARANTEED TO AROUSE INTEREST AND STIR DESIRE.

*The light and
subtle flavors of
a succulent seafood
and avocado salad will
appeal to Geminians.*

- THE FOOD OF LOVE -

FOR ARIENS
Spicy mulligatawny soup
·
Peppered steak
·
Baked Alaska

FOR TAUREANS
Cream of cauliflower soup
·
Tournedos Rossini
·
Rich chocolate and brandy mousse

FOR GEMINIANS
Seafood and avocado salad
·
Piquant stir-fried pork with ginger
·
Zabaglione

FOR CANCERIANS
Artichoke vinaigrette
·
Sole Bonne Femme
·
Almond soufflé

– THE FOOD OF LOVE –

FOR LEOS

Roasted tomato and garlic soup

·

Boeuf Stroganoff

·

Pears cooked in wine

FOR VIRGOS

Eggplant salad

·

Paella

·

French apple tart

FOR LIBRANS

Asparagus with hollandaise sauce

Pork with roasted apples

Strawberry Pavlova

FOR SCORPIOS

Vichyssoise

·

Lobster Newburg

·

Blueberry cream

– THE FOOD OF LOVE –

FOR SAGITTARIANS
Chilled cucumber soup
·
Nutty onion flan
·
Rhubarb crumble with fresh cream

FOR CAPRICORNS
Eggs Florentine
·
Pork tenderloin stuffed with sage
·
Pineapple Pavlova

FOR AQUARIANS
Watercress soup
·
Chicken cooked with chili and lime
·
Lemon soufflé

FOR PISCEANS
French onion soup
·
Trout au vin rosé
·
Melon sorbet

PLACES TO LOVE

ONCE YOU HAVE WON YOUR LOVER'S HEART, A ROMANTIC
VACATION TOGETHER WILL SEAL YOUR LOVE. HERE, YOU
CAN DISCOVER THE PERFECT DESTINATION FOR EACH SUN
SIGN, FROM HISTORIC CITIES TO IDYLLIC BEACHES.

ARIES

*Florence is an Arien
city, and its perfectly
preserved Renaissance
palaces and churches
will set the scene for
wonderful romance.*

GEMINI

*Vivacious and restless
Geminians will feel at
home in the fast-paced
and sophisticated
atmosphere of
New York.*

TAURUS

*The unspoiled scenery
and unhurried pace
of life in rural Ireland
is sure to appeal to
patient and placid
Taureans.*

CANCER

*The watery beauty
and uniquely romantic
atmosphere of Venice
is guaranteed to arouse
passion and stir the
Cancerian imagination.*

THE
EIFFEL
TOWER,
PARIS

ST. BASIL'S
CATHEDRAL,
MOSCOW

AYERS ROCK/ULURU,
AUSTRALIA

LEO

*Leos will fall in love
all over again when
surrounded by the
picturesque charm and
unspoiled medieval
atmosphere of Prague.*

VIRGO

*Perhaps the most
elegant and romantic
of all cities, Paris is
certainly the ideal
setting for a stylish and
fastidious Virgo.*

LIBRA

*The dramatic and
exotic beauty of Upper
Egypt and the Nile will
provide the perfect
backdrop for wooing
a romantic Libran.*

SCORPIO

*Intense and passionate
Scorpios will be strongly
attracted by the whiff
of danger present in
the exotic atmosphere
of New Orleans.*

SAGITTARIUS

*The wide-ranging
spaces of the Australian
outback will appeal
to the Sagittarian love
of freedom and the
great outdoors.*

CAPRICORN

*Capricorns will be
fascinated and inspired
by the great historical
monuments of Moscow,
the most powerful of all
Russian cities.*

AQUARIUS

*Intrepid Aquarians will
be enthralled and
amazed by the unusual
sights and spectacular
landscapes of the
Indian subcontinent.*

PISCES

*Water-loving Pisceans
will be at their most
relaxed and romantic
by the sea, perhaps on
a small and unspoiled
Mediterranean island.*

THE PYRAMIDS,
EGYPT

GONDOLAS,
VENICE

THE TAJ MAHAL,
INDIA

VENUS & MARS

LUCID, SHINING VENUS AND FIERY, RED MARS HAVE ALWAYS BEEN
ASSOCIATED WITH HUMAN LOVE AND PASSION. THE TWO
PLANETS HAVE A POWERFUL INFLUENCE ON OUR ATTITUDES
TOWARD LOVE, SEX, AND RELATIONSHIPS.

*T*he study of astrology first began long before humankind began to record its own history. The earliest astrological artifacts discovered, scratches on bones recording the phases of the Moon, date from well before the invention of any alphabet or writing system.

The planets Venus and Mars have always been regarded as having enormous significance in astrology. This is evident from the tentative attempts of early astrologers to record the effects of the two planets on humankind. Hundreds of years later, the positions of the planets were carefully noted in personal horoscopes. The earliest known record is dated 410 BC: "Venus [was] in the Bull, and Mars in the Twins."

The bright, shining planet Venus represents the gentle effect of the soul on our physical lives. It is responsible for a refined and romantic sensuality – "pure" love, untainted by sex. Venus reigns over our attitudes toward romance and the spiritual dimension of love.

The planet Mars affects the physical aspects of our lives – our strength, both physical and mental; our endurance; and our ability to fight for survival. Mars is also strongly linked to the sex drive of both men and women. Mars governs our physical energy, sexuality, and levels of desire.

Venus is known as an "inferior" planet, because its orbit falls between Earth and the Sun. Venus orbits the Sun

LOVE CONQUERS ALL

In Botticelli's Venus and Mars, *the warlike, fiery
energy of Mars, the god of war, has been overcome by
the gentle charms of Venus, the goddess of love.*

closely, and its position in the zodiac is always in a sign near that of the Sun. As a result, the planet can only have occupied one of five given signs at the time of your birth – your Sun sign, or the two signs before or after it. For example, if you were born with the Sun in Virgo, Venus can only have occupied Cancer, Leo, Virgo, Libra, or Scorpio at that moment.

Mars, on the other hand, is a "superior" planet. Its orbit lies on the other side of Earth from the Sun, and therefore the planet may have occupied any of the 12 signs at the moment of your birth.

On the following pages (24–45) we provide you with fascinating insights into how Mars and Venus govern your attitudes toward love, sex, and relationships. To ascertain which sign of the zodiac the planets occupied at the moment of your birth, you must first consult the tables on pages 52–61. Then turn to page 24 and read on.

YOUR LOVE LIFE

THE PLANET VENUS REPRESENTS LOVE, HARMONY, AND UNITY.
WORK OUT WHICH SIGN OF THE ZODIAC VENUS OCCUPIED AT
THE MOMENT OF YOUR BIRTH (SEE PAGES 52–57), AND READ ON.

VENUS IN ARIES

*T*his planetary placing will heighten your emotions, which will have a positive effect. Geminians can be a little cool, and tend to bottle up their feelings, but you should have no such problems. You are likely to be a good communicator and will find it easy to discuss your emotions openly.

You are inclined to fall in love very swiftly, and will be eager to make an eloquent declaration of love to your prospective partner. However, you may find that he or she will appreciate a romantic gesture or love letter more than an impassioned torrent of words promising undying devotion. Remember that actions speak louder than words and can have a more immediate effect.

You may try to persuade any potential partners into a serious relationship before they are quite ready. As a result, they can feel pressured and back away. Try to subdue your Arien impatience, for such an attitude can appear impulsive and overly hasty.

When Venus shines from this sign, a dash of Arien spice adds strength of feeling to the Geminian personality. You may be hot-tempered and volatile, with a tendency to fly into a rage. Unless your partner is equally tempestuous, you may intimidate him or her by the heat of your emotions. If in danger of losing your temper, count to ten and remember that the provocative influence of Venus is responsible for your fieriness.

Geminians make entertaining, lively companions, but are not always easy to live with. You have an impatient side to your personality. Be careful not to snap at your partner if he or she is being a little slow on the uptake, or having difficulty in making a decision. You may also display a hint of Arien selfishness by always putting yourself first. Try to restrain these less attractive qualities.

Intelligent and perceptive, Geminians are well suited to a partner who can challenge and entertain them. They have questioning minds, and are invigorated by incisive discussion and debate. An intellectual rapport between you and your lover is very important to you. If your partner cannot stimulate your mind, you may become bored and turn to illicit affairs to enliven your existence.

VENUS IN TAURUS

From Taurus, Venus brings you a capacity for simple and straightforward affection. Geminians do not have a high emotional temperature, but this placing will make it easier for you to express your love warmly and honestly. The influence of Venus will bring you down to earth, and you will be a generous and affectionate partner.

When Venus shines from Taurus, the planet can increase your levels of physical attraction and bring you a great deal of charm. When these qualities are combined with the high spirits and vivacity so characteristic of Gemini, you will have no difficulty in attracting admirers, and they will find you both desirable and interesting.

Geminians often leap into an affair at the first sign of interest. You will revel in the excitement of seduction and courtship.

However, once this stage has passed and you have become involved in a permanent alliance, you may become restless, turning to illicit affairs for excitement. Fortunately, any Gemininan unfaithfulness will be lessened by the influence of Venus from this sign. Due to the sincere and faithful qualities of Taurus, infidelity will be easy to resist.

You are an entertaining and lively companion, and your effusive enjoyment of life is infectious. Friendship is just as important to you as romance, and your perfect partner will be someone with whom you can share your many enthusiasms and interests – a companion as well as a lover. If you and your partner share an intellectual rapport, your relationship will satisfy and stimulate you both mentally and physically, and you will be much less likely to turn to infidelity to inject a little excitement into your life.

The typically Taurean delight in sensuality and luxury will be conveyed by Venus when it shines from Taurus, and you will want to woo your potential partner in comfort and style.

However, Venus may also bring a less attractive Taurean trait – possessiveness. This destructive emotion is usually alien to lighthearted and freedom-loving Geminians, but if you were born with Venus in Taurus it may manifest itself in your character. Do not allow a claustrophobic or restrictive atmosphere to pervade your relationship, because it could cause great damage. Your partner may feel that you are becoming too intense and be scared away. If you suffer any sudden pangs of possessiveness, try to quell them with the help of your rational and coolheaded Geminian qualities.

VENUS IN GEMINI

*T*hose born when both the Sun and Venus occupied Gemini will find that all their typically Geminian qualities are heightened. Your provocative flirtatiousness and your capacity for deceit and infidelity will be increased, and you may yearn for the thrill of affairs and secret liaisons.

You are quick-witted and lively, with a talent for creating a sense of friendship within your relationship. However, unless you feel you are on the same intellectual wavelength as your partner, your affair will not last long. You also need variety and experimentation in your sex life, and any prudishness or excessive conventionality on the part of your lover will prove irritating.

Geminians thrive on flirtation and illicit entanglements, and struggle with the concept of absolute fidelity to one partner.

It is difficult for you to comprehend why people are so critical of infidelity. To you, a quick fling is just harmless and unimportant fun, no more than a natural response to a physical urge. You tend to find it hard to understand your partner's pain when you are unfaithful. You may not be very sympathetic to your lover's feelings of betrayal, feeling that he or she is making a fuss about nothing. You will expect your partner to understand that your love has not diminished, and that your physical unfaithfulness poses no real threat to your relationship.

Geminians are vivacious and gregarious. Eternally popular, your social calendar will be packed full of engagements, and you can be the life and soul of the party. Quiet evenings in with your partner do not hold much appeal for you, because you are in your element in a social situation.

An insecure partner or one who is prone to jealousy may feel threatened by your love of company. Try to understand that not everyone is as sociable as you are, and that your partner will sometimes want your complete attention.

Gemini is ruled by Mercury, the planet of communication. You will be eloquent and articulate, and should find it easy to talk things through with your partner. You have a persuasive manner and will use all your Geminian ingenuity to wriggle out of a corner when confronted with infidelity. Your lover may be deceived by your excuses, but in the end you must admit to your misdemeanors. Unless your partner is remarkably easygoing and tolerant, your tendency to play the field will probably have to lessen if your relationship is to succeed.

VENUS IN CANCER

*V*enus in Cancer will boost your capacity for love and affection, and you will make a loyal and tender lover.

From Cancer, Venus will raise your emotional temperature considerably. This is a very beneficial influence, as Sun-sign Geminians tend to be rather unemotional and detached. However, with this placing you will be a demonstrative and affectionate lover, lavishing attentions on your partner.

Home is the center of the Cancerian universe, and if Venus occupied Cancer at the moment of your birth, you will probably be a devoted homemaker. Your natural instinct is to care for and cherish your partner and family, and to create a happy and harmonious home. Your home is a refuge from the stresses and strains of day-to-day life, and it will possess a calm and tranquil atmosphere.

Due to the influence of Cancer, a stable and secure relationship will be very important to you. However, because you are still a Sun-sign Geminian, you will possess a tendency toward infidelity and deceit. You may experience a sense of inner conflict when your home-loving Cancerian instinct battles with your proclivity for illicit liaisons.

The Cancerian influence from Venus can make you very nostalgic, and you may view the past through rose-colored glasses, however content you are in your present-day life. This yearning for "the good old days" may result in self-indulgent reminiscing. However, your Geminian love of novelty should counter your fear of change and encourage you to regard the future positively.

The influence of Cancer may bring you a possessive streak. This is very out of character

for a Geminian, and you may deplore this failing in yourself, but it will prove difficult to control. A potentially splendid relationship could be warped by this destructive emotion; therefore, you must strive to overcome any signs of jealousy or possessiveness.

With Venus shining from Cancer, you may be rather abrupt. When this quality is combined with your Geminian impatience, you may find that you become easily irritated. If your partner is occasionally slow on the uptake or dawdles when you are in a hurry, you may become exasperated and lash out at him or her verbally. Your quick Geminian tongue can be acerbic and may do more damage than intended; therefore, if you feel irritated, count to ten, take a deep breath, and try to remain patient.

VENUS IN LEO

*W*hen Venus occupies Leo, all your passionate emotions will be focused on your partner. You are a very supportive lover, spurring your loved one on and enthusiastically encouraging this person to attain all his or her ambitions. Do not become too commanding, or you may end up bullying a partner who you feel is not achieving full potential.

Due to the influence of Leo, you enjoy good living and will want to lavish all the trappings of luxury on your lover. Leos are extravagant and Geminians are usually generous with their money; they find the idea of economy and frugality boring and unattractive. As a result, your affairs can burn up more money than you realize and you may find yourself overspending. Try to adopt a responsible approach, or you may find yourself getting into financial difficulties. Luckily, your generosity will be emotional as well as financial, and you are able to express your feelings in words as well as deeds. You may even discover that your partner appreciates your sincere declarations of love much more than expensive gifts.

With Venus in Leo at the moment of your birth, you will be less likely to enter into illicit involvements. Leonine loyalty will combat Geminian duality, and you are more likely to remain faithful to your lover than many other Geminians. However, you will still be an accomplished flirt, and may be tempted into the occasional affair. If your infidelity is discovered, you may argue that your liaison was unimportant. However, you value faithfulness in your partner very highly and will find it difficult to forgive or forget a lover's indulgence in an affair.

A partner who is unfaithful to you will damage your self-esteem and make you feel humiliated.

Your chances of remaining faithful to your partner will be greatly increased if you can find a lover who is as sexually active and imaginative as you are. When Venus shines from passionate Leo, your capacity for sexual enjoyment and experimentation will be greatly increased. Your sex life must be exciting and adventurous if it is to retain your interest and fulfill your desires.

Both Leo and Gemini are sociable signs, and when Venus is in Leo you will be popular and congenial. You have a warm, sincere personality and find it easy to talk to anyone. With this planetary placement, you will never be a loner – you will be in your natural element at social gatherings and celebrations.

YOUR SEX LIFE

THE PLANET MARS REPRESENTS PHYSICAL AND SEXUAL ENERGY.
WORK OUT WHICH SIGN OF THE ZODIAC MARS OCCUPIED AT THE
MOMENT OF YOUR BIRTH (SEE PAGES 58–61), AND READ ON.

MARS IN ARIES

From Aries, Mars will bring you a very high level of physical energy and will boost your sex drive. As a result, you will be an ardent and rewarding lover as well as an adventurous and inspiring companion.

Geminians can find the concept of sexual fidelity hard to grasp, and sexual jealousy and possessiveness are a mystery to them. Your Geminian restlessness, combined with your strong Arien sexuality, may tempt you to a string of affairs.

Your partner is likely to find your careless attitude to sexual fidelity hard to endure. Do not allow your unfaithfulness to destroy your relationship.

MARS IN TAURUS

Mars from Taurus will imbue you with a generous and warmhearted passion. If you were born with this planetary placing, you are likely to be very much in touch with your body and physical needs, and will have a healthy, uncomplicated sexual appetite. You are uninhibited and totally at ease with your body.

If Mars occupied Taurus at the moment of your birth, you will find it much easier than your fellow Geminians to control your wandering eye. The solid and steadfast influence of Taurus will help to counteract the Geminian tendency to infidelity.

You are hardworking and diligent, and your Taurean determination will give you the ability to plod on when others might give up. Your perseverance will prove to be helpful if you are attracted to someone who initially rebuffs your approaches. Keep on trying, and your natural charm should eventually win this person over.

MARS IN GEMINI

*W*hen Mars and the Sun share the same sign, all your Geminian traits will be intensified. Your charming words and vivacious and witty personality will attract many potential lovers.

You need a varied and exciting sex life, and if your lover does not possess similar levels of sexual energy and desire, your interest will not be held for very long. Your long-term affairs must be kept alive by plenty of novelty and diversity.

The Geminian tendency toward infidelity will be emphasized by this placing, and you may find it difficult to remain faithful to one partner. Your Geminian restlessness may lead you into illicit affairs and intrigue.

Be warned – infidelity will almost certainly damage your long-term relationships. You may try to convince your partner that an occasional fling means nothing to you, but most people will find it very hard to endure your constant unfaithfulness.

MARS IN CANCER

*T*he Cancerian influence will make you a splendidly caring and sensuous lover, and anyone who enters into an affair with you is likely to feel very fortunate indeed.

Due to the influence of Cancer, you will be more committed to domesticity and home life than many Geminians. The sign should dampen any urges toward infidelity. Once you have completely committed yourself to someone you are unlikely to stray.

From Cancer, Mars will bring you tenacity and resolution. You will be determined to capture anyone on whom you set your sights. Try not to make your pursuit too forceful or impatient, or you could frighten your lover away.

You are sexually passionate and revel in the physical expression of your love, but a string of affairs will not appeal to you. A secure and affectionate relationship is your ideal and you will work hard to attain it.

– YOUR SEX LIFE –

MARS IN LEO

*M*ars and Leo work well together, instilling in you a great zest for life and a dynamic sexuality. Your sex life is guaranteed to be lively, and your ardor may even prove exhausting to anyone with a less powerful sex drive.

You are likely to adopt a relaxed approach to the subject of sexual fidelity. You may argue that brief affairs are unimportant and therefore should not affect your permanent relationship. You have a tendency to write off any objections to your romantic intrigues and flirtations as narrowmindedness and petty intolerance. However, your partner is unlikely to be impressed by this argument.

You have an abundance of physical energy, and excel at all forms of exercise – including sexual activity. Your dynamism will also manifest itself in your excellent organization skills. These will certainly come in handy if you find yourself juggling any illicit affairs.

MARS IN VIRGO

*T*his placing will bring you nervous energy, and an ambiguous attitude to sex.

If Mars occupied Virgo at the moment of your birth, you will be very hardworking and will put great effort into making your partnership work.

Virgos are both fastidious and modest – qualities that can inhibit the vivid sexuality of Mars. Although you possess all the sensuality typical of an Earth sign, you may be reserved when it comes to expressing it.

Your Geminian duality may clash with the shyness and modesty that Mars can bring from Virgo. This will be a beneficial influence, as a casual and careless attitude to fidelity will not help forge a happy and secure relationship.

The nervous energy of Virgo can make you tense and prone to stress. Relaxation techniques can be helpful. Your sex life could be greatly improved if you and your partner practice techniques such as sensual massage together.

MARS IN LIBRA

$\mathcal{D}$ue to the influence of Libra you will be eager to form a long-lasting relationship and will be less likely to indulge in illicit affairs. You will be a sensual lover, but may be lazy when it comes to initiating sexual activity. Your lover will not know whether to expect an exciting night of passion or a chaste cup of cocoa.

The Libran influence may make you indecisive. If the influence of Gemini tempts you to begin an affair, you will agonize over whether or not to go ahead with it. However, you will be more of a romantic idealist than many of your fellow Geminians, and the thought of infidelity may make you uneasy.

You are highly romantic, and tend to fall in love with the very idea of being in love. This will combine with your Geminian need for constant novelty and excitement, with the result that you may find yourself falling madly in love with someone new every other week.

– YOUR SEX LIFE –

MARS IN SCORPIO

Traditionally, Mars is said to "rule" Scorpio, and from this sign the planet intensifies your sexuality. If your partner cannot satisfy your vigorous sexual demands, your strong sex drive, combined with your Geminian duality, may tempt you to seek out a series of lovers. Even when you are involved in a sexually fulfilling relationship, the occasional fling may occur.

Geminians are not often prone to jealousy, and the very concept of this emotion is quite alien to them. However, Mars works powerfully from Scorpio, and may introduce the green-eyed monster into your life.

Such a negative and wasteful emotion is unlikely to gain a permanent foothold in your personality, but you will realize that jealousy is a very powerful emotion, and that it can cause great pain. This awareness will be beneficial if it deters you from indulging the flirtatious Geminian side of your character in front of your partner.

MARS IN SAGITTARIUS

*W*hen Mars shines from Sagittarius it will provide Geminians with an extra burst of energy. You will be excited by the prospect of illicit liaisons and sexual escapades, and Sagittarius will provide you with the stamina to indulge in as many relationships as you want.

You have an excess of physical energy and will thrive on excitement and adventure. Danger may excite you, but instead of taking risks, channel your energy into achieving your ambitions. Geminians can be restless, and this influence may be increased by Sagittarius. Therefore, you may need to force yourself to carry your projects through to completion.

Once you have satisfied your appetite for affairs and intrigue, you may begin to think about finding a permanent partner. You will have no difficulty in finding an eager candidate, for you are an exciting and versatile lover who enjoys exploring new and different areas of lovemaking.

MARS IN CAPRICORN

*M*ars and Capricorn are so fundamentally different that this placing may cause some inner conflict. Mars is fiery and impetuous – a total contrast to the prudent qualities of earthy Capricorn.

However, this placing can prove highly beneficial. The disciplined influence of Capricorn will steady your restless Geminian emotions and bring you a greater degree of self-control. Your libido will be cooled by Mars in Capricorn, but you will still have

considerable physical stamina, and your lover will not be able to accuse you of laziness when it comes to your sex life.

From Capricorn, Mars will bring you great strength of character, and once you have set your sights on someone, your flattering determination to win their heart will soon bowl them over. However, you will not hurry into a relationship; your innate sense of caution encourages you to look carefully before you leap.

MARS IN AQUARIUS

From Aquarius, Mars brings a need for solitude and independence. These qualities will combine with your innate Geminian flirtatiousness. As a result, you will want to retain a degree of freedom in your relationships, allowing you to play the field despite the fact that you are already committed to someone. However, unlike many Geminians, you will not indulge in clandestine intrigues and secret affairs, because openness and honesty are important to you.

You treasure your freedom; therefore, long-term commitment may be hard for you. However, once you have taken the plunge and become involved in a permanent relationship, you are extremely loyal and faithful.

Aquarian sexuality is not famous for its vigor or intensity, but you enjoy sex and are a versatile and stimulating lover. You will be considerate and altruistic, eager to ensure that your lover enjoys just as much pleasure as you do.

- YOUR SEX LIFE -

MARS IN PISCES

*M*ars from Pisces will introduce a veritable torrent of emotion into your cool Geminian personality. Your levels of passion will be increased, and you will make a sensitive and stimulating lover.

Due to the Piscean influence, you will be romantic and sensual, but your sexuality may not be very highly charged. However, your imaginative and poetic approach to sex can be far more erotic than boundless physical stamina.

Sexual passion means much more to you than uncomplicated fun and physical release. It can assume an almost spiritual dimension and provide you with a means of attaining true communion with your partner. This idealistic approach to your sexuality is truly seductive.

With this placing of Mars, there can be a tendency toward self-deception and secrecy. Try to be open and honest with your lover, because this will greatly benefit your relationship.

TOKENS OF LOVE

ASTROLOGY CAN GIVE YOU A FASCINATING INSIGHT INTO YOUR
LOVER'S PERSONALITY AND ATTITUDE TOWARD LOVE. IT CAN
ALSO PROVIDE YOU WITH SOME INVALUABLE HINTS WHEN YOU
WANT TO CHOOSE THE PERFECT GIFT FOR YOUR LOVER.

GOLF TEES

ARIES
*Ariens tend to be very
active and energetic,
and sports equipment
is guaranteed
to please.*

CRYSTALLIZED
CHESTNUTS

TAURUS
*Delicately scented pot-
pourri or an elegant,
comfortable cushion will
delight a Taurean lover.*

GEMINI
*A handsome box
of exotic nuts or
Jordan almonds
will be appreciated
by a Geminian.*

POT-
POURRI
POMANDER

HEART-
SHAPED
SOAP

CANCER

*Cancerians take good
care of their skin, and
luxurious soap will be
appreciated.
Cancer is ruled
by the moon,
and any item
with a moon
motif is sure
to please.*

ENAMELED PILLBOX
WITH MOON
MOTIF

GOLDEN CROWN
ORNAMENT

WILDFLOWER
HONEY

LEO

*Leos love colorful
and flamboyant items.
Anything gold or gold-
colored is sure to
delight a Leo. The Sun
is Leo's ruling planet,
and therefore any
objects with a sun
motif will appeal
to your Leo lover.*

REGENCY-
STYLE CHAIR

VIRGO

*Any objects
made from wood
will appeal to
Virgos because
they are drawn to
natural materials.
A health-conscious
Virgoan lover will
prefer a jar of
wildflower honey
to a large box
of chocolates.*

– TOKENS OF LOVE –

LIBRA

Librans are true romantics. They love music of all kinds, and will be enraptured by a recording of their favorite piece.

VIOLIN

SCORPIO

The opal is the Scorpio birthstone and makes an ideal gift. A handsome lamp will occupy pride of place in a Scorpio home.

BLACK OPALS

TABLE LAMP

VICTORIAN TRAVEL BOOKS

SAGITTARIUS

Adventurous Sagittarians love to travel, and travel books and accessories will be greatly appreciated.

– TOKENS OF LOVE –

CAPRICORN

Only the best, such as a fine glass decanter or a traditional umbrella, will appeal to the taste of a fastidious Capricorn.

WAXED COTTON
UMBRELLA WITH
DECORATED
INTERIOR

GLASS
GOBLET

AQUARIUS

Aquarians adore unusual gifts. Beautiful hand-blown modern glass is guaranteed to please.

ANTIQUE GLASS
DECANTER

THAI SILK
SCARF

PISCES

Soft and sumptuous silks and velvets will suit sensual Pisceans – choose a flowing silk scarf or a plump velvet cushion for them.

GIVING A BIRTHSTONE

The most personal gift you can give your lover is the gem linked to his or her Sun sign.

AGATE

ARIES: *diamond*
TAURUS: *emerald*
GEMINI: *agate* • CANCER: *pearl*
LEO: *ruby* • VIRGO: *sardonyx*
LIBRA: *sapphire* • SCORPIO: *opal*
SAGITTARIUS: *topaz*
CAPRICORN: *amethyst*
AQUARIUS: *aquamarine*
PISCES: *moonstone*

YOUR PERMANENT RELATIONSHIP

GEMINIANS LOVE NOVELTY AND CHANGE. TO ENSURE A
SUCCESSFUL AND SECURE PERMANENT RELATIONSHIP, STRONG
TIES OF FRIENDSHIP WITH YOUR PARTNER ARE ESSENTIAL.

Geminians are characterized by their charm and their seductive flirtatiousness, and their roving eye may cause their partners some problems. Your high spirits make you a lively companion, and you are likely to be the center of attention at any gathering. However, while your flirtatious charm is focused on someone else, your lover may be suffering pangs of jealousy.

To many Geminians, flirting merely represents harmless fun. However, your lover may not appreciate this, and the sight of your thoughtless philandering may wound them just as much as an all-out affair. Remember to reassure them of your love, and try to keep your roving eye under control.

Life with a Geminian will never be dull. You are likely to dislike anything that smacks of the commonplace or ordinary, but remember that for some people security, safety, and routine are important. Try to understandthis and make allowances when your partner pales with horrorat the news that you have given up your job so that you can both bicycle around the world.

However, it is not only your lover who needs a measure of serenity and relaxation. Even you need to enjoy a little peace and quiet from time to time. Geminians sometimes find it difficult to relax – hopefully, your lover will be able to teach you this happy art.

A JOINT FUTURE
On a Sailing Ship, *by Caspar David Friedrich, shows a newly married couple sailing into a bright but unknown future together.*

Your ruling planet is Mercury, which encourages good communication, and you will find it easy to communicate with your partner. You will be eager to talk through any problems that arise in your relationship, and if you can persuade your partner to be equally candid, you will resolve any problems through honest discussion.

You are unlikely to make emotional scenes, but your quick tongue can be very scathing. Try not to speak too hastily, as sharp words may hurt your partner more than you intended.

Geminians tend to be restless; therefore, you and your partner should share common interests. They will keep your relationship alive and flourishing long after the initial passion and ardor has died down and sex has assumed a rather less dominant role.

VENUS & MARS TABLES

THESE TABLES WILL ENABLE YOU TO DISCOVER WHICH SIGNS
VENUS AND MARS OCCUPIED AT THE MOMENT OF YOUR BIRTH.
TURN TO PAGES 24–45 TO INVESTIGATE THE QUALITIES OF THESE
SIGNS, AND TO FIND OUT HOW THEY WORK WITH YOUR SUN SIGN.

The tables on pages 53–61 will enable you to discover the positions of Venus and Mars at the moment of your birth.

First find your year of birth on the top line of the appropriate table, then find your month of birth in the left-hand column. Where the column for your year of birth intersects with the row for your month of birth, you will find a group of figures and zodiacal glyphs. These figures and glyphs show which sign of the zodiac the planet occupied on the first day of that month, and any date during that month on which the planet moved into another sign.

For example, to ascertain the position of Venus on May 10, 1968, run your finger down the column marked 1968 until you reach the row for May. The row of numbers and glyphs shows that Venus occupied Aries on May 1, entered Taurus on May 4, and then moved into Gemini on May 28. Therefore, on May 10, Venus was in Taurus.

If you were born on a day when one of the planets was moving into a new sign, it may be impossible to determine your Venus and Mars signs completely accurately. If the characteristics described on the relevant pages do not seem to apply to you, read the interpretation of the sign before and after. One of these signs will be appropriate.

ZODIACAL GLYPHS			
♈	Aries	♎	Libra
♉	Taurus	♏	Scorpio
♊	Gemini	♐	Sagittarius
♋	Cancer	♑	Capricorn
♌	Leo	♒	Aquarius
♍	Virgo	♓	Pisces

– VENUS TABLES –

♀	1921	1922	1923	1924	1925	1926	1927	1928
JAN	1♒ 7♓	1♑ 25♒	1♏ 3♐	1♒ 20♓	1♐ 15♑	1♒	1♑ 10♒	1♏ 5♐ 30♑
FEB	1♓ 3♈	1♒ 18♓	1♐ 7♑ 14♒	1♓ 14♈	1♑ 8♒	1♒	1♒ 3♓ 27♈	1♑ 23♒
MAR	1♈ 8♉	1♓ 14♈	1♑ 7♒	1♈ 10♉	1♒ 5♓ 29♈	1♒	1♈ 23♉	1♒ 19♓
APR	1♉ 26♈	1♈ 7♉	1♒ 2♓ 27♈	1♉ 8♊	1♈ 22♉	1♈ 7♉	1♉ 17♊	1♓ 12♈
MAY	1♈	1♉ 2♊ 26♋	1♈ 22♉	1♊ 7♋	1♉ 16♊	1♉ 7♊	1♊ 13♋	1♈ 7♉ 31♊
JUN	1♈ 3♉	1♋ 20♌	1♉ 16♊	1♋	1♊ 10♋	1♊ 3♋ 29♊	1♋ 9♌	1♊ 24♋
JUL	1♉ 9♊	1♌ 16♍	1♊ 11♋	1♋	1♋ 4♌ 29♍	1♊ 25♋	1♌ 8♍	1♋ 19♌
AUG	1♊ 6♋	1♍ 11♎	1♋ 4♌ 28♍	1♋	1♍ 23♎	1♋ 19♌	1♍	1♌ 12♍
SEP	1♌ 27♍	1♎ 8♏	1♍ 22♎	1♋ 8♌	1♎ 17♏	1♌ 12♍	1♍	1♍ 5♎ 30♏
OCT	1♍ 21♎	1♏ 11♐	1♎ 16♏	1♌ 7♍	1♏ 12♐	1♍ 6♎ 30♏	1♍	1♏ 24♐
NOV	1♎ 14♏	1♐ 29♑	1♏ 9♐	1♍ 3♎ 28♏	1♏ 7♐	1♏ 23♐	1♍ 10♎	1♐ 18♑
DEC	1♏ 8♐	1♑	1♐ 3♑ 27♒	1♏ 22♐	1♐ 6♑	1♐ 17♑	1♎ 9♏	1♑ 13♒

♀	1929	1930	1931	1932	1933	1934	1935	1936
JAN	1♒ 7♓	1♑ 25♒	1♏ 4♐	1♒ 20♓	1♐ 15♑	1♒	1♑ 9♒	1♏ 4♐ 29♑
FEB	1♓ 3♈	1♒ 17♓	1♐ 7♑	1♓ 13♈	1♑ 8♒	1♒	1♒ 2♓ 27♈	1♑ 23♒
MAR	1♈ 9♉	1♓ 14♈	1♑ 6♒	1♈ 10♉	1♒ 4♓ 28♈	1♒	1♈ 23♉	1♒ 18♓
APR	1♉ 21♈	1♈ 7♉	1♒ 27♈	1♉ 6♊	1♈ 21♉	1♈ 7♉	1♉ 17♊	1♓ 12♈
MAY	1♈	1♊ 26♋	1♈ 22♉	1♊ 7♋	1♉ 16♊	1♉ 7♊	1♊ 12♋	1♈ 6♉ 30♊
JUN	1♈ 4♉	1♋ 20♌	1♉ 15♊	1♋	1♊ 9♋	1♊	1♋ 8♌	1♊ 24♋
JUL	1♉ 9♊	1♌ 15♍	1♊ 10♋	1♋ 14♌ 29♋	1♋ 4♌ 28♍	1♊ 24♋	1♌ 8♍	1♋ 18♌
AUG	1♊ 6♋	1♍ 11♎	1♋ 4♌ 28♍	1♋	1♍ 22♎	1♋ 18♌	1♍	1♌ 12♍
SEP	1♌ 26♍	1♎ 8♏	1♍ 21♎	1♋ 9♌	1♎ 16♏	1♌ 12♍	1♍	1♍ 5♎ 29♏
OCT	1♍ 21♎	1♏ 13♐	1♎ 15♏	1♌ 8♍	1♏ 12♐	1♍ 6♎ 30♏	1♍	1♏ 24♐
NOV	1♎ 14♏	1♐ 23♑	1♏ 8♐	1♍ 3♎ 28♏	1♐ 7♑	1♏ 23♐	1♍ 10♎	1♐ 17♑
DEC	1♏ 8♐ 31♑	1♑	1♐ 2♑ 26♒	1♏ 22♐	1♑ 6♒	1♐ 17♑	1♎ 9♏	1♑ 12♒

♀	1937	1938	1939	1940	1941	1942	1943	1944
JAN	1 ♒ · 7 ♓	1 ♑ · 24 ♒	1 ♏ · 5 ♐	1 ♐ · 19 ♑	1 ♒ · 14 ♓	1 ♒	1 ♑ · 9 ♒	1 ♏ · 4 ♐ · 29 ♑
FEB	1 ♓ · 3 ♈	1 ♒ · 17 ♓	1 ♐ · 7 ♑	1 ♓ · 13 ♈	1 ♒ · 7 ♓	1 ♒	1 ♒ · 2 ♓ · 26 ♈	1 ♑ · 22 ♒
MAR	1 ♈ · 10 ♉	1 ♓ · 13 ♈	1 ♑ · 6 ♒	1 ♈ · 9 ♉	1 ♒ · 3 ♓ · 28 ♈	1 ♒	1 ♈ · 22 ♉	1 ♒ · 18 ♓
APR	1 ♉ · 15 ♈	1 ♈ · 6 ♉ · 30 ♊	1 ♓ · 26 ♈	1 ♉ · 5 ♊	1 ♈ · 21 ♉	1 ♒ · 7 ♓	1 ♉ · 7 ♊	1 ♓ · 11 ♈
MAY	1 ♈	1 ♊ · 25 ♋	1 ♈ · 21 ♉	1 ♉ · 7 ♊	1 ♉ · 15 ♊	1 ♓ · 7 ♈	1 ♊ · 12 ♋	1 ♈ · 5 ♉ · 30 ♊
JUN	1 ♈ · 5 ♉	1 ♋ · 19 ♌	1 ♉ · 15 ♊	1 ♋	1 ♊	1 ♈ · 8 ♉ · 28 ♊	1 ♊ · 23 ♋	1 ♊ · 23 ♋
JUL	1 ♉ · 8 ♊	1 ♌ · 15 ♍	1 ♊ · 10 ♋	1 ♋ · 6 ♊	1 ♋ · 3 ♌ · 28 ♍	1 ♊ · 24 ♋	1 ♋ · 8 ♌	1 ♋ · 18 ♌
AUG	1 ♊ · 5 ♋	1 ♍ · 10 ♎	1 ♋ · 3 ♌ · 27 ♍	1 ♊ · 2 ♋	1 ♍ · 22 ♎	1 ♋ · 18 ♌	1 ♌	1 ♌ · 11 ♍
SEP	1 ♌ · 26 ♍	1 ♎ · 8 ♏	1 ♍ · 21 ♎	1 ♋ · 9 ♌	1 ♎ · 16 ♍	1 ♌ · 11 ♍	1 ♌	1 ♍ · 4 ♎ · 29 ♏
OCT	1 ♍ · 20 ♎	1 ♏ · 14 ♐	1 ♎ · 15 ♏	1 ♌ · 7 ♍	1 ♍ · 11 ♎	1 ♍ · 5 ♎ · 29 ♏	1 ♍	1 ♏ · 23 ♐
NOV	1 ♎ · 13 ♏	1 ♐ · 16 ♏	1 ♏ · 8 ♐	1 ♍ · 2 ♎ · 27 ♏	1 ♎ · 7 ♐	1 ♏ · 22 ♐	1 ♎ · 22 ♍	1 ♐ · 17 ♑
DEC	1 ♏ · 7 ♐ · 31 ♑	1 ♏	1 ♐ · 2 ♑ · 26 ♒	1 ♏ · 21 ♐	1 ♐ · 6 ♑	1 ♐ · 16 ♑	1 ♎ · 9 ♏	1 ♑ · 12 ♒

♀	1945	1946	1947	1948	1949	1950	1951	1952
JAN	1 ♒ · 6 ♓	1 ♑ · 23 ♒	1 ♏ · 6 ♐	1 ♐ · 19 ♑	1 ♐ · 14 ♑	1 ♒	1 ♑ · 8 ♒	1 ♏ · 3 ♐ · 28 ♑
FEB	1 ♓ · 3 ♈	1 ♒ · 16 ♓	1 ♐ · 7 ♑	1 ♒ · 12 ♓	1 ♑ · 7 ♒	1 ♒	1 ♑ · 25 ♒	1 ♒ · 21 ♓
MAR	1 ♈ · 12 ♉	1 ♓ · 12 ♈	1 ♑ · 6 ♒ · 31 ♓	1 ♓ · 9 ♈	1 ♒ · 3 ♓ · 27 ♈	1 ♒	1 ♈ · 22 ♉	1 ♒ · 17 ♓
APR	1 ♉ · 8 ♈	1 ♈ · 6 ♉ · 30 ♊	1 ♓ · 26 ♈	1 ♈ · 26 ♉	1 ♈ · 20 ♉	1 ♒ · 7 ♓	1 ♉ · 16 ♊	1 ♓ · 10 ♈
MAY	1 ♈	1 ♊ · 25 ♋	1 ♈ · 21 ♉	1 ♉ · 8 ♊	1 ♉ · 15 ♊	1 ♈ · 6 ♉	1 ♊ · 12 ♋	1 ♈ · 5 ♉ · 29 ♊
JUN	1 ♈ · 5 ♉	1 ♋ · 19 ♌	1 ♉ · 14 ♊	1 ♊ · 30 ♋	1 ♊ · 30 ♋	1 ♉ · 2 ♊ · 28 ♋	1 ♊ · 23 ♋	1 ♊ · 23 ♋
JUL	1 ♉ · 8 ♊	1 ♌ · 14 ♍	1 ♊ · 9 ♋	1 ♊	1 ♋ · 2 ♌ · 27 ♍	1 ♊ · 23 ♋	1 ♊ · 9 ♋	1 ♋ · 17 ♌
AUG	1 ♊ · 5 ♋ · 31 ♌	1 ♍ · 10 ♎	1 ♋ · 3 ♌ · 27 ♍	1 ♊ · 4 ♋	1 ♍ · 21 ♎	1 ♋ · 17 ♌	1 ♍	1 ♌ · 10 ♍
SEP	1 ♌ · 25 ♍	1 ♎ · 8 ♏	1 ♍ · 20 ♎	1 ♊ · 9 ♋	1 ♎ · 15 ♍	1 ♌ · 11 ♍	1 ♍	1 ♍ · 4 ♎ · 28 ♏
OCT	1 ♍ · 20 ♎	1 ♏ · 17 ♐	1 ♎ · 14 ♏	1 ♋ · 7 ♌	1 ♍ · 11 ♎	1 ♍ · 5 ♎ · 29 ♏	1 ♍	1 ♏ · 23 ♐
NOV	1 ♎ · 13 ♏	1 ♐ · 9 ♏	1 ♏ · 7 ♐	1 ♌ · 2 ♍ · 27 ♎	1 ♎ · 7 ♐	1 ♏ · 22 ♐	1 ♍ · 2 ♎	1 ♐ · 16 ♑
DEC	1 ♏ · 7 ♐ · 31 ♑	1 ♏	1 ♐ · 25 ♑	1 ♎ · 21 ♏	1 ♏ · 7 ♐	1 ♐ · 15 ♑	1 ♎ · 9 ♏	1 ♑ · 11 ♒

– VENUS TABLES –

♀	1953	1954	1955	1956	1957	1958	1959	1960
JAN	1 ♒ 6 ♓	1 ♑ 23 ♒	1 ♏ 7 ♐	1 ♒ 18 ♓	1 ♏ 13 ♐	1 ♐ ♑	1 ♑ 8 ♒	1 ♏ 3 ♐ 28 ♑
FEB	1 ♓ 3 ♈	1 ♒ 16 ♓	1 ♐ 7 ♑	1 ♓ 12 ♈	1 ♐ 6 ♑	1 ♒	1 ♓ 25 ♈	1 ♑ 21 ♒
MAR	1 ♈ 15 ♉	1 ♓ 12 ♈	1 ♑ 5 ♒ 31 ♓	1 ♈ 8 ♉	1 ♑ 2 ♒ 26 ♓	1 ♒	1 ♈ 21 ♉	1 ♒ 16 ♓
APR	1 ♈	1 ♈ 5 ♉ 29 ♊	1 ♓ 25 ♈	1 ♉ 5 ♊	1 ♓ 19 ♈	1 ♒ 7 ♓	1 ♉ 15 ♊	1 ♓ 10 ♈
MAY	1 ♈	1 ♊ 24 ♋	1 ♈ 20 ♉	1 ♊ 9 ♋	1 ♈ 14 ♉	1 ♓ 6 ♈	1 ♊ 11 ♋	1 ♈ 4 ♉ 29 ♊
JUN	1 ♈ 6 ♉	1 ♋ 18 ♌	1 ♉ 14 ♊	1 ♋ 24 ♊	1 ♉ 7 ♊	1 ♈ 7 ♉	1 ♋ 22 ♌	1 ♊ 22 ♋
JUL	1 ♉ 8 ♊	1 ♌ 14 ♍	1 ♊ 9 ♋	1 ♊	1 ♋ 27 ♌	1 ♉ 22 ♊	1 ♌ 9 ♍	1 ♋ 16 ♌
AUG	1 ♊ 5 ♋ 31 ♌	1 ♍ 10 ♎	1 ♋ 2 ♌ 26 ♍	1 ♊ 5 ♋	1 ♌ 21 ♍	1 ♊ 16 ♋	1 ♍	1 ♌ 9 ♍
SEP	1 ♌ 25 ♍	1 ♎ 7 ♏	1 ♍ 19 ♎	1 ♋ 9 ♌	1 ♍ 15 ♎	1 ♋ 10 ♌	1 ♍ 21 ♎ 26 ♍	1 ♍ 3 ♎ 28 ♏
OCT	1 ♍ 19 ♎	1 ♏ 24 ♐ 28 ♏	1 ♎ 13 ♏	1 ♌ 7 ♍	1 ♎ 11 ♏	1 ♌ 3 ♍ 28 ♎	1 ♍	1 ♏ 22 ♐
NOV	1 ♎ 12 ♏	1 ♏	1 ♏ 6 ♐	1 ♍ 26 ♎	1 ♏	1 ♎ 21 ♏	1 ♍ 10 ♎	1 ♐ 16 ♑
DEC	1 ♏ 6 ♐ 30 ♑	1 ♏	1 ♐ 25 ♑	1 ♎ 20 ♏	1 ♏ 7 ♐	1 ♏ 15 ♐	1 ♎ 8 ♏	1 ♑ 11 ♒

♀	1961	1962	1963	1964	1965	1966	1967	1968
JAN	1 ♒ 6 ♓	1 ♑ 22 ♒	1 ♏ 7 ♐	1 ♒ 17 ♓	1 ♏ 13 ♐	1 ♒	1 ♑ 7 ♒ 31 ♓	1 ♏ 2 ♐ 27 ♑
FEB	1 ♓ 3 ♈	1 ♒ 15 ♓	1 ♐ 6 ♑	1 ♓ 11 ♈	1 ♐ 6 ♑	1 ♒ 7 ♑ 26 ♒	1 ♓ 24 ♈	1 ♑ 21 ♒
MAR	1 ♈	1 ♓ 11 ♈	1 ♑ 5 ♒ 31 ♓	1 ♈ 8 ♉	1 ♑ 2 ♒ 26 ♓	1 ♒	1 ♈ 21 ♉	1 ♒ 16 ♓
APR	1 ♈	1 ♈ 4 ♉ 29 ♊	1 ♓ 25 ♈	1 ♉ 5 ♊	1 ♓ 19 ♈	1 ♒ 7 ♓	1 ♉ 15 ♊	1 ♓ 9 ♈
MAY	1 ♈	1 ♊ 24 ♋	1 ♈ 19 ♉	1 ♊ 10 ♋	1 ♈ 13 ♉	1 ♓ 6 ♈	1 ♊ 11 ♋	1 ♈ 4 ♉ 28 ♊
JUN	1 ♈ 6 ♉	1 ♋ 18 ♌	1 ♉ 13 ♊	1 ♋ 18 ♊	1 ♉ 7 ♊	1 ♈ 27 ♉	1 ♋	1 ♊ 21 ♋
JUL	1 ♉ 8 ♊	1 ♌ 13 ♍	1 ♊ 8 ♋	1 ♊	1 ♋ 26 ♌	1 ♉ 22 ♊	1 ♋ 9 ♌	1 ♋ 16 ♌
AUG	1 ♊ 4 ♋ 30 ♌	1 ♍ 9 ♎	1 ♌ 26 ♍	1 ♊ 6 ♋	1 ♌ 20 ♍	1 ♊ 16 ♋	1 ♌	1 ♌ 9 ♍
SEP	1 ♌ 24 ♍	1 ♎ 8 ♏	1 ♍ 18 ♎	1 ♋ 9 ♌	1 ♍ 14 ♎	1 ♋ 9 ♌	1 ♌ 10 ♍	1 ♍ 3 ♎ 27 ♏
OCT	1 ♍ 18 ♎	1 ♏	1 ♎ 13 ♏	1 ♌ 6 ♍	1 ♎ 10 ♏	1 ♌ 3 ♍ 27 ♎	1 ♍ 2 ♌	1 ♏ 22 ♐
NOV	1 ♎ 12 ♏	1 ♏	1 ♏ 6 ♐ 30 ♑	1 ♍ 25 ♎	1 ♏ 6 ♐	1 ♎ 20 ♏	1 ♌ 10 ♍	1 ♐ 15 ♑
DEC	1 ♏ 6 ♐ 29 ♑	1 ♏	1 ♑ 24 ♒	1 ♎ 20 ♏	1 ♐ 8 ♑	1 ♏ 14 ♐	1 ♍ 8 ♎	1 ♑ 10 ♒

♀	1969	1970	1971	1972	1973	1974	1975	1976
JAN	1 ♒ 5 ♓	1 ♑ 22 ♒	1 ♏ 8 ♐	1 ♒ 17 ♓	1 ♐ 12 ♑	1 ♒ 30 ♑	1 ♑ 7 ♒ 31 ♓	1 ♏ 2 ♐ 27 ♑
FEB	1 ♓ 3 ♈	1 ♒ 15 ♓	1 ♐ 6 ♑	1 ♓ 11 ♈	1 ♑ 5 ♒	1 ♒	1 ♓ 24 ♈	1 ♑ 20 ♒
MAR	1 ♈	1 ♓ 11 ♈	1 ♑ 5 ♒ 30 ♓	1 ♈ 8 ♉	1 ♓ 25 ♈	1 ♒	1 ♈ 20 ♉	1 ♒ 15 ♓
APR	1 ♈	1 ♈ 4 ♉ 28 ♊	1 ♓ 24 ♈	1 ♉ 4 ♊	1 ♈ 19 ♉	1 ♒ 7 ♓	1 ♉ 14 ♊	1 ♓ 9 ♈
MAY	1 ♈	1 ♊ 23 ♋	1 ♈ 19 ♉	1 ♊ 11 ♋	1 ♉ 13 ♊	1 ♓ 5 ♈	1 ♊ 10 ♋	1 ♈ 3 ♉ 27 ♊
JUN	1 ♈ 6 ♉	1 ♋ 17 ♌	1 ♉ 13 ♊	1 ♋ 12 ♊	1 ♊ 6 ♋	1 ♉ 26 ♊	1 ♋ 7 ♌	1 ♊ 21 ♋
JUL	1 ♉ 7 ♊	1 ♌ 13 ♍	1 ♊ 7 ♋	1 ♊	1 ♌ 26 ♍	1 ♊ 22 ♋	1 ♌ 10 ♍	1 ♋ 15 ♌
AUG	1 ♊ 4 ♋ 30 ♌	1 ♍ 9 ♎	1 ♌ 25 ♍	1 ♊ 7 ♋	1 ♍ 19 ♎	1 ♋ 15 ♌	1 ♍	1 ♌ 9 ♍
SEP	1 ♌ 24 ♍	1 ♎ 8 ♏	1 ♍ 18 ♎	1 ♋ 8 ♌	1 ♎ 14 ♍	1 ♌ 9 ♍	1 ♍ 3 ♎	1 ♍ 2 ♎ 26 ♏
OCT	1 ♍ 18 ♎	1 ♏	1 ♎ 12 ♏	1 ♌ 6 ♍ 31 ♎	1 ♍ 10 ♎	1 ♍ 3 ♎ 27 ♏	1 ♎ 5 ♍	1 ♏ 21 ♐
NOV	1 ♎ 11 ♏	1 ♏	1 ♏ 5 ♐ 30 ♑	1 ♎ 25 ♏	1 ♐ 6 ♑	1 ♏ 20 ♐	1 ♍ 10 ♎	1 ♐ 15 ♑
DEC	1 ♏ 5 ♐ 29 ♑	1 ♏	1 ♑ 24 ♒	1 ♏ 19 ♐	1 ♑ 8 ♒	1 ♐ 14 ♑	1 ♎ 7 ♏	1 ♑ 10 ♒

♀	1977	1978	1979	1980	1981	1982	1983	1984
JAN	1 ♒ 5 ♓	1 ♑ 21 ♒	1 ♏ 8 ♐	1 ♒ 16 ♓	1 ♐ 12 ♑	1 ♒ 24 ♑	1 ♑ 6 ♒ 30 ♓	1 ♏ 2 ♐ 26 ♑
FEB	1 ♓ 3 ♈	1 ♒ 14 ♓	1 ♐ 6 ♑	1 ♓ 10 ♈	1 ♑ 5 ♒ 28 ♓	1 ♑	1 ♓ 23 ♈	1 ♑ 20 ♒
MAR	1 ♈	1 ♓ 10 ♈	1 ♑ 4 ♒ 29 ♓	1 ♈ 7 ♉	1 ♓ 25 ♈	1 ♑ 3 ♒	1 ♈ 20 ♉	1 ♒ 15 ♓
APR	1 ♈	1 ♈ 3 ♉ 28 ♊	1 ♓ 23 ♈	1 ♉ 4 ♊	1 ♈ 18 ♉	1 ♒ 7 ♓	1 ♉ 14 ♊	1 ♓ 8 ♈
MAY	1 ♈	1 ♊ 22 ♋	1 ♈ 18 ♉	1 ♊ 13 ♋	1 ♉ 12 ♊	1 ♓ 5 ♈ 31 ♉	1 ♊ 10 ♋	1 ♈ 3 ♉ 27 ♊
JUN	1 ♈ 7 ♉	1 ♋ 17 ♌	1 ♉ 12 ♊	1 ♋ 6 ♊	1 ♉ 6 ♊ 30 ♋	1 ♉ 26 ♊	1 ♋ 7 ♌	1 ♊ 21 ♋
JUL	1 ♉ 7 ♊	1 ♌ 12 ♍	1 ♊ 7 ♋ 31 ♌	1 ♊	1 ♋ 25 ♌	1 ♊ 21 ♋	1 ♌ 11 ♍	1 ♋ 15 ♌
AUG	1 ♊ 3 ♋ 29 ♌	1 ♍ 8 ♎	1 ♌ 25 ♍	1 ♊ 7 ♋	1 ♍ 19 ♎	1 ♋ 15 ♌	1 ♍ 28 ♌	1 ♌ 8 ♍
SEP	1 ♌ 23 ♍	1 ♎ 8 ♏	1 ♍ 18 ♎	1 ♋ 8 ♌	1 ♎ 13 ♍	1 ♌ 8 ♍	1 ♌	1 ♍ 2 ♎ 26 ♏
OCT	1 ♍ 17 ♎	1 ♏	1 ♎ 12 ♏	1 ♌ 5 ♍ 31 ♎	1 ♍ 9 ♎	1 ♍ 2 ♎ 26 ♏	1 ♌ 6 ♍	1 ♏ 21 ♐
NOV	1 ♎ 11 ♏	1 ♏	1 ♏ 5 ♐ 29 ♑	1 ♎ 25 ♏	1 ♐ 6 ♑	1 ♏ 19 ♐	1 ♍ 10 ♎	1 ♐ 14 ♑
DEC	1 ♏ 4 ♐ 28 ♑	1 ♏	1 ♑ 23 ♒	1 ♏ 19 ♐	1 ♑ 9 ♒	1 ♐ 12 ♑	1 ♎ 7 ♏	1 ♑ 10 ♒

- VENUS TABLES -

♀	1985	1986	1987	1988	1989	1990	1991	1992
JAN	1 ♒ 5 ♓	1 ♑ 21 ♒	1 ♏ 8 ♐	1 ♒ 16 ♓	1 ♐ 11 ♑	1 ♒ 17 ♑	1 ♑ 6 ♒ 30 ♓	1 ♐ 26 ♑
FEB	1 ♓ 3 ♈	1 ♒ 14 ♓	1 ♐ 6 ♑	1 ♓ 10 ♈	1 ♑ 4 ♒ 28 ♓	1 ♑	1 ♓ 23 ♈	1 ♑ 19 ♒
MAR	1 ♈	1 ♓ 9 ♈	1 ♑ 4 ♒ 29 ♓	1 ♈ 7 ♉	1 ♓ 24 ♈	1 ♑ 4 ♒	1 ♈ 19 ♉	1 ♒ 14 ♓
APR	1 ♈	1 ♈ 3 ♉ 27 ♊	1 ♓ 23 ♈	1 ♉ 4 ♊	1 ♈ 17 ♉	1 ♒ 7 ♓	1 ♉ 13 ♊	1 ♓ 7 ♈
MAY	1 ♈	1 ♊ 22 ♋	1 ♈ 18 ♉	1 ♊ 18 ♋ 27 ♊	1 ♉ 12 ♊	1 ♓ 4 ♈ 31 ♉	1 ♊ 9 ♋	1 ♈ 2 ♉ 26 ♊
JUN	1 ♈ 7 ♉	1 ♋ 16 ♌	1 ♉ 12 ♊	1 ♊	1 ♊ 5 ♋ 30 ♌	1 ♉ 25 ♊	1 ♋ 7 ♌	1 ♊ 20 ♋
JUL	1 ♉ 7 ♊	1 ♌ 12 ♍	1 ♊ 6 ♋ 31 ♌	1 ♊	1 ♌ 24 ♍	1 ♊ 20 ♋	1 ♌ 11 ♍	1 ♋ 14 ♌
AUG	1 ♊ 3 ♋ 28 ♌	1 ♍ 24 ♎	1 ♌ 24 ♍	1 ♊ 7 ♋	1 ♍ 18 ♎	1 ♋ 13 ♌	1 ♍ 22 ♎	1 ♌ 7 ♍
SEP	1 ♌ 23 ♍	1 ♎ 8 ♏	1 ♍ 17 ♎	1 ♋ 8 ♌	1 ♌ 13 ♍	1 ♌ 9 ♍	1 ♌	1 ♍ 25 ♎
OCT	1 ♍ ♎	1 ♏	1 ♎ 11 ♏	1 ♌ 5 ♍ 30 ♎	1 ♏ ♐	1 ♍ 2 ♎ 26 ♏	1 ♌ 7 ♍	1 ♏ 20 ♐
NOV	1 ♎ 10 ♏	1 ♏	1 ♏ 4 ♐ 28 ♑	1 ♎ 24 ♏	1 ♐ 6 ♑	1 ♏ 19 ♐	1 ♍ 9 ♎	1 ♐ 14 ♑
DEC	1 ♏ 4 ♐ 28 ♑	1 ♏	1 ♑ 23 ♒	1 ♏ 18 ♐	1 ♑ 10 ♒	1 ♐ 13 ♑	1 ♎ 7 ♏	1 ♑ 9 ♒

♀	1993	1994	1995	1996	1997	1998	1999	2000
JAN	1 ♒ 4 ♓	1 ♑ 20 ♒	1 ♏ 8 ♐	1 ♒ 15 ♓	1 ♐ 10 ♑	1 ♒ 10 ♑	1 ♑ 5 ♒ 29 ♓	1 ♐ 25 ♑
FEB	1 ♓ 3 ♈	1 ♒ 13 ♓	1 ♐ 5 ♑	1 ♓ 9 ♈	1 ♑ 4 ♒ 28 ♓	1 ♑	1 ♓ 22 ♈	1 ♑ 19 ♒
MAR	1 ♈	1 ♓ 9 ♈	1 ♑ 3 ♒ 29 ♓	1 ♈ 6 ♉	1 ♓ 24 ♈	1 ♑ 5 ♒	1 ♈ 19 ♉	1 ♒ 14 ♓
APR	1 ♈	1 ♈ 2 ♉ 27 ♊	1 ♓ 23 ♈	1 ♉ 4 ♊	1 ♈ 17 ♉	1 ♒ 7 ♓	1 ♉ 13 ♊	1 ♓ 7 ♈
MAY	1 ♈	1 ♊ 21 ♋	1 ♈ 17 ♉	1 ♊	1 ♉ 11 ♊	1 ♓ 4 ♈ 30 ♉	1 ♊ 9 ♋	1 ♈ 2 ♉ 26 ♊
JUN	1 ♈ 7 ♉	1 ♋ 15 ♌	1 ♉ 11 ♊	1 ♊	1 ♊ 4 ♋ 29 ♌	1 ♉ 25 ♊	1 ♋ 6 ♌	1 ♊ 19 ♋
JUL	1 ♉ 6 ♊	1 ♌ 12 ♍	1 ♊ 6 ♋ 30 ♌	1 ♊	1 ♌ 24 ♍	1 ♊ 20 ♋	1 ♌ 13 ♍	1 ♋ 14 ♌
AUG	1 ♊ 2 ♋ 28 ♌	1 ♍ 8 ♎	1 ♌ 23 ♍	1 ♊ 8 ♋	1 ♍ 18 ♎	1 ♋ 14 ♌	1 ♍ 16 ♎	1 ♌ 7 ♍
SEP	1 ♌ 22 ♍	1 ♎ 8 ♏	1 ♍ 17 ♎	1 ♋ 8 ♌	1 ♌ 12 ♍	1 ♌ 7 ♍	1 ♌	1 ♍ 25 ♎
OCT	1 ♍ 16 ♎	1 ♏	1 ♎ 11 ♏	1 ♌ 5 ♍ 30 ♎	1 ♎ 9 ♏	1 ♍ 25 ♎	1 ♌ 8 ♍	1 ♏ 20 ♐
NOV	1 ♎ 9 ♏	1 ♏	1 ♏ 4 ♐ 28 ♑	1 ♎ 23 ♏	1 ♐ 6 ♑	1 ♏ 18 ♐	1 ♍ 10 ♎	1 ♐ 13 ♑
DEC	1 ♏ 3 ♐ 27 ♑	1 ♏	1 ♑ 22 ♒	1 ♏ 17 ♐	1 ♑ 12 ♒	1 ♐ 12 ♑	1 ♎ 6 ♏	1 ♑ 9 ♒

♂	1921	1922	1923	1924	1925	1926	1927	1928	1929	1930
JAN	1 ♒ 5 ♓	1 ♏	1 ♓ 21 ♈	1 ♏ 19 ♐	1 ♈	1 ♐	1 ♉	1 ♐ 19 ♑	1 ♊	1 ♑
FEB	1 ♓ 13 ♈	1 ♏ 18 ♐	1 ♈	1 ♐	1 ♈ 5 ♉	1 ♐ 9 ♑	1 ♉ 22 ♊	1 ♑ 28 ♒	1 ♊	1 ♑ 6 ♒
MAR	1 ♈ 25 ♉	1 ♐	1 ♈ 4 ♉	1 ♐ 6 ♑	1 ♉ 24 ♊	1 ♑ 23 ♒	1 ♊	1 ♒	1 ♊ 10 ♋	1 ♒ 17 ♓
APR	1 ♉	1 ♐	1 ♉ 16 ♊	1 ♑ 24 ♒	1 ♊	1 ♒	1 ♊ 17 ♋	1 ♒ 7 ♓	1 ♋	1 ♓ 24 ♈
MAY	1 ♉ 6 ♊	1 ♐	1 ♊ 30 ♋	1 ♒	1 ♊ 9 ♋	1 ♒ 3 ♓	1 ♋	1 ♓ 16 ♈	1 ♋ 13 ♌	1 ♈
JUN	1 ♊ 18 ♋	1 ♐	1 ♋	1 ♒ 24 ♓	1 ♋ 26 ♌	1 ♓ 15 ♈	1 ♋ 6 ♌	1 ♈ 26 ♉	1 ♌	1 ♈ 3 ♉
JUL	1 ♋	1 ♐	1 ♋ 16 ♌	1 ♓	1 ♌	1 ♈	1 ♌ 25 ♍	1 ♉	1 ♌ 4 ♍	1 ♉ 14 ♊
AUG	1 ♋ 3 ♌	1 ♐	1 ♌	1 ♓ 24 ♒	1 ♌ 12 ♍	1 ♉	1 ♍	1 ♉ 9 ♊	1 ♍ 21 ♎	1 ♊ 28 ♋
SEP	1 ♌ 19 ♍	1 ♐ 13 ♑	1 ♍	1 ♒	1 ♍ 28 ♎	1 ♉	1 ♍ 10 ♎	1 ♊	1 ♎	1 ♋
OCT	1 ♍	1 ♑ 30 ♒	1 ♍ 18 ♎	1 ♒ 19 ♓	1 ♎	1 ♉	1 ♎ 26 ♏	1 ♊ 3 ♋	1 ♎ 6 ♏	1 ♋ 20 ♌
NOV	1 ♍ 6 ♎	1 ♒	1 ♎	1 ♓	1 ♎ 13 ♏	1 ♉	1 ♏	1 ♋	1 ♏ 18 ♐	1 ♌
DEC	1 ♎ 26 ♏	1 ♒ 11 ♓	1 ♎ 4 ♏	1 ♓ 19 ♈	1 ♏ 28 ♐	1 ♉	1 ♏ 8 ♐	1 ♋ 20 ♊	1 ♐ 29 ♑	1 ♌

♂	1931	1932	1933	1934	1935	1936	1937	1938	1939	1940
JAN	1 ♌	1 ♑ 18 ♒	1 ♍	1 ♒	1 ♎	1 ♒ 14 ♓	1 ♎ 5 ♏	1 ♓ 30 ♈	1 ♏ 29 ♐	1 ♓ 4 ♈
FEB	1 ♌ 16 ♋	1 ♒ 25 ♓	1 ♍	1 ♒ 4 ♓	1 ♎	1 ♓ 22 ♈	1 ♏	1 ♈	1 ♐	1 ♈ 17 ♉
MAR	1 ♋ 30 ♌	1 ♓	1 ♍	1 ♓ 14 ♈	1 ♎	1 ♈	1 ♏ 13 ♐	1 ♈ 12 ♉	1 ♐ 21 ♑	1 ♉
APR	1 ♌	1 ♓ 3 ♈	1 ♍	1 ♈ 22 ♉	1 ♎	1 ♉	1 ♐	1 ♉ 23 ♊	1 ♑	1 ♊
MAY	1 ♌	1 ♈ 12 ♉	1 ♍	1 ♉	1 ♎	1 ♉ 13 ♊	1 ♐ 14 ♏	1 ♊	1 ♑ 25 ♒	1 ♊ 17 ♋
JUN	1 ♌ 10 ♍	1 ♉ 22 ♊	1 ♍	1 ♉ 2 ♊	1 ♎	1 ♊ 25 ♋	1 ♏	1 ♊ 7 ♋	1 ♒	1 ♋
JUL	1 ♍	1 ♊	1 ♍ 6 ♎	1 ♊ 15 ♋	1 ♎ 29 ♏	1 ♋	1 ♏	1 ♋ 22 ♌	1 ♒ 21 ♑	1 ♋ 3 ♌
AUG	1 ♎	1 ♊ 4 ♋	1 ♎ 26 ♏	1 ♋ 30 ♌	1 ♏	1 ♋ 10 ♌	1 ♏ 8 ♐	1 ♌	1 ♑	1 ♌ 19 ♍
SEP	1 ♎ 17 ♏	1 ♋ 20 ♌	1 ♏	1 ♌	1 ♏ 16 ♐	1 ♌ 26 ♍	1 ♐ 30 ♑	1 ♌ 7 ♍	1 ♑ 24 ♒	1 ♍
OCT	1 ♏ 30 ♐	1 ♌	1 ♏ 9 ♐	1 ♌ 18 ♍	1 ♐ 28 ♑	1 ♍	1 ♑	1 ♍ 25 ♎	1 ♒	1 ♍ 5 ♎
NOV	1 ♐	1 ♌ 13 ♍	1 ♐ 19 ♑	1 ♍	1 ♑	1 ♍ 14 ♎	1 ♑ 11 ♒	1 ♎	1 ♒ 19 ♓	1 ♎ 20 ♏
DEC	1 ♐ 10 ♑	1 ♍	1 ♑ 28 ♒	1 ♍ 11 ♎	1 ♑ 7 ♒	1 ♎	1 ♒ 21 ♓	1 ♎ 11 ♏	1 ♓	1 ♏

– MARS TABLES –

♂	1941	1942	1943	1944	1945	1946	1947	1948	1949	1950
JAN	1 ♏ 4 ♐	1 ♈ 11 ♉	1 ♐ 26 ♑	1 ♊	1 ♐ 5 ♑	1 ♋	1 ♑ 25 ♒	1 ♍	1 ♑ 4 ♒	1 ♎
FEB	1 ♐ 17 ♑	1 ♉	1 ♑	1 ♊	1 ♑ 14 ♒	1 ♋	1 ♒	1 ♍ 12 ♌	1 ♒ 11 ♓	1 ♎
MAR	1 ♑	1 ♉ 7 ♊	1 ♑ 8 ♒	1 ♊ 29 ♋	1 ♒ 25 ♓	1 ♋	1 ♒ 4 ♓	1 ♌	1 ♓ 21 ♈	1 ♎ 28 ♍
APR	1 ♑ 2 ♒	1 ♊ 26 ♋	1 ♒ 17 ♓	1 ♋	1 ♓	1 ♋ 22 ♌	1 ♓ 11 ♈	1 ♌	1 ♈ 30 ♉	1 ♍
MAY	1 ♒ 16 ♓	1 ♋	1 ♓ 27 ♈	1 ♋ 22 ♌	1 ♓ 3 ♈	1 ♌	1 ♈ 21 ♉	1 ♌ 18 ♍	1 ♉	1 ♍
JUN	1 ♓	1 ♋ 14 ♌	1 ♈	1 ♌	1 ♈ 11 ♉	1 ♌ 20 ♍	1 ♉	1 ♍	1 ♉ 10 ♊	1 ♍ 11 ♎
JUL	1 ♓ 2 ♈	1 ♌	1 ♈ 7 ♉	1 ♌ 12 ♍	1 ♉ 23 ♊	1 ♍	1 ♊	1 ♍ 17 ♎	1 ♊ 23 ♋	1 ♎
AUG	1 ♈	1 ♍	1 ♉ 23 ♊	1 ♍ 29 ♎	1 ♊	1 ♍ 9 ♎	1 ♊ 13 ♋	1 ♎	1 ♋	1 ♎ 10 ♏
SEP	1 ♈	1 ♍ 17 ♎	1 ♊	1 ♎	1 ♊ 7 ♋	1 ♎ 24 ♏	1 ♋	1 ♎ 3 ♏	1 ♋ 7 ♌	1 ♏ 25 ♐
OCT	1 ♈	1 ♎	1 ♊	1 ♎ 13 ♏	1 ♋	1 ♏	1 ♌	1 ♏ 17 ♐	1 ♌ 27 ♍	1 ♐
NOV	1 ♈	1 ♎ 2 ♏	1 ♊	1 ♏ 25 ♐	1 ♋ 11 ♌	1 ♏ 6 ♐	1 ♌	1 ♐ 26 ♑	1 ♍	1 ♐ 6 ♑
DEC	1 ♈	1 ♏ 15 ♐	1 ♊	1 ♐	1 ♌ 26 ♋	1 ♐ 17 ♑	1 ♍	1 ♑	1 ♍ 26 ♎	1 ♑ 15 ♒

♂	1951	1952	1953	1954	1955	1956	1957	1958	1959	1960
JAN	1 ♒ 22 ♓	1 ♎ 20 ♏	1 ♓	1 ♏	1 ♓ 15 ♈	1 ♏ 14 ♐	1 ♈ 28 ♉	1 ♐	1 ♉	1 ♐ 14 ♑
FEB	1 ♓	1 ♏	1 ♓ 8 ♈	1 ♏ 9 ♐	1 ♈ 26 ♉	1 ♐ 28 ♑	1 ♉	1 ♐ 3 ♑	1 ♉ 10 ♊	1 ♑ 23 ♒
MAR	1 ♓ 2 ♈	1 ♏	1 ♈ 20 ♉	1 ♐	1 ♉	1 ♑	1 ♉ 17 ♊	1 ♑ 17 ♒	1 ♊	1 ♒
APR	1 ♈ 10 ♉	1 ♏	1 ♉	1 ♐ 12 ♑	1 ♉ 10 ♊	1 ♑ 14 ♒	1 ♊	1 ♒ 27 ♓	1 ♊ 10 ♋	1 ♒ 2 ♓
MAY	1 ♉ 21 ♊	1 ♏	1 ♊	1 ♑	1 ♊ 26 ♋	1 ♒	1 ♊ 4 ♋	1 ♓	1 ♋	1 ♓ 11 ♈
JUN	1 ♊	1 ♏	1 ♊ 14 ♋	1 ♑	1 ♋	1 ♒ 3 ♓	1 ♋ 21 ♌	1 ♓ 7 ♈	1 ♋ 21 ♌	1 ♈ 20 ♉
JUL	1 ♊ 3 ♋	1 ♏	1 ♋ 29 ♌	1 ♑ 3 ♐	1 ♋ 11 ♌	1 ♓	1 ♌	1 ♈ 21 ♉	1 ♌	1 ♉
AUG	1 ♋ 18 ♌	1 ♏ 27 ♐	1 ♌	1 ♐ 24 ♑	1 ♌ 27 ♍	1 ♓	1 ♌ 8 ♍	1 ♉	1 ♌	1 ♉ 8 ♊
SEP	1 ♌	1 ♐	1 ♌ 14 ♍	1 ♑	1 ♍	1 ♓	1 ♍ 24 ♎	1 ♉ 21 ♊	1 ♌ 5 ♍	1 ♊ 21 ♋
OCT	1 ♌ 5 ♍	1 ♐ 12 ♑	1 ♍	1 ♑ 21 ♒	1 ♍ 13 ♎	1 ♓	1 ♎	1 ♊ 21 ♉	1 ♍ 21 ♎	1 ♋
NOV	1 ♍ 24 ♎	1 ♑ 21 ♒	1 ♍ 21 ♎	1 ♒	1 ♎ 29 ♏	1 ♓	1 ♎ 8 ♏	1 ♉	1 ♎	1 ♋
DEC	1 ♎	1 ♒ 30 ♓	1 ♎ 20 ♏	1 ♒ 4 ♓	1 ♏	1 ♓ 6 ♈	1 ♏ 23 ♐	1 ♉	1 ♏ 3 ♐	1 ♋

♂	1961	1962	1963	1964	1965	1966	1967	1968	1969	1970
JAN	1 ♋	1 ♑	1 ♌	1 13 ♑ ♒	1 ♏	1 30 ♒ ♓	1 ♎	1 9 ♒ ♓	1 ♏	1 24 ♓ ♈
FEB	1 5 7 ♋ ♊ ♋	1 2 ♑ ♒	1 ♌	1 20 ♒ ♓	1 ♏	1 ♓	1 12 ♎ ♏	1 17 ♓ ♈	1 25 ♏ ♐	1 ♈
MAR	1 ♋	1 12 ♒ ♓	1 ♌	1 29 ♓ ♈	1 ♏	1 9 ♓ ♈	1 31 ♏ ♎	1 28 ♈ ♉	1 ♐	1 7 ♈ ♉
APR	1 ♋	1 19 ♓ ♈	1 ♌	1 ♈	1 ♏	1 17 ♈ ♉	1 ♎	1 ♉	1 ♐	1 18 ♉ ♊
MAY	1 6 ♋ ♌	1 28 ♈ ♉	1 ♌	1 7 ♈ ♉	1 ♏	1 28 ♉ ♊	1 ♎	1 8 ♉ ♊	1 ♐	1 ♊
JUN	1 28 ♌ ♍	1 ♉	1 3 ♌ ♍	1 ♉ ♊	1 29 ♍ ♎	1 ♊	1 ♎	1 21 ♊ ♋	1 ♐	1 2 ♊ ♋
JUL	1 ♍	1 9 ♉ ♊	1 27 ♍ ♎	1 30 ♊ ♋	1 ♎	1 11 ♊ ♋	1 19 ♎ ♏	1 ♋	1 ♐	1 18 ♋ ♌
AUG	1 17 ♍ ♎	1 22 ♊ ♋	1 ♎	1 ♋	1 ♋	1 20 ♋ ♏	1 25 ♋ ♌	1 ♍	1 5 ♋ ♌	1 ♌
SEP	1 ♎	1 ♋	1 12 ♎ ♏	1 15 ♋ ♌	1 ♌	1 ♌	1 10 ♏ ♐	1 21 ♌ ♍	1 21 ♐ ♑	1 3 ♌ ♍
OCT	1 2 ♎ ♏	1 11 ♋ ♌	1 25 ♏ ♐	1 ♌	1 4 ♍ ♐	1 12 ♌ ♍	1 23 ♐ ♑	1 ♍	1 ♑	1 20 ♍ ♎
NOV	1 13 ♏ ♐	1 ♌	1 ♐	1 6 ♌ ♍	1 14 ♐ ♑	1 ♍	1 ♑	1 9 ♍ ♎	1 4 ♑ ♒	1 ♎
DEC	1 24 ♐ ♑	1 ♌	1 5 ♐ ♑	1 ♍	1 23 ♑ ♒	1 4 ♍ ♎	1 2 ♑ ♒	1 30 ♍ ♏	1 15 ♒ ♓	1 6 ♍ ♏

♂	1971	1972	1973	1974	1975	1976	1977	1978	1979	1980
JAN	1 23 ♏ ♐	1 ♈	1 ♐	1 ♉	1 21 ♐ ♑	1 ♊	1 ♑	1 26 ♌ ♋	1 ♑ ♒	1 ♍
FEB	1 ♐	1 10 ♈ ♉	1 12 ♐ ♑	1 27 ♉ ♊	1 ♑	1 ♊	1 9 ♑ ♒	1 ♋	1 28 ♒ ♓	1 ♍
MAR	1 12 ♐ ♑	1 27 ♉ ♊	1 27 ♑ ♒	1 ♊	1 3 ♑ ♒	1 18 ♊ ♋	1 20 ♒ ♓	1 ♋	1 ♓	1 12 ♍ ♌
APR	1 ♑	1 ♊	1 ♒	1 20 ♊ ♋	1 11 ♒ ♓	1 ♋	1 28 ♓ ♈	1 11 ♋ ♌	1 7 ♓ ♈	1 ♌
MAY	1 3 ♑ ♒	1 12 ♊ ♋	1 8 ♒ ♓	1 ♋	1 21 ♓ ♈	1 16 ♋ ♌	1 ♈	1 ♌	1 16 ♈ ♉	1 4 ♌ ♍
JUN	1 ♒	1 28 ♋ ♌	1 21 ♓ ♈	1 9 ♋ ♌	1 ♈	1 ♌	1 6 ♈ ♉	1 14 ♌ ♍	1 26 ♉ ♊	1 ♍
JUL	1 ♒	1 ♌	1 ♈	1 27 ♌ ♍	1 ♉	1 ♌	1 7 ♌ ♍	1 18 ♉ ♊	1 ♊	1 11 ♍ ♎
AUG	1 ♒	1 15 ♌ ♍	1 12 ♈ ♉	1 ♍	1 14 ♉ ♊	1 24 ♌ ♍	1 ♍	1 4 ♍ ♎	1 8 ♊ ♋	1 29 ♍ ♏
SEP	1 ♒	1 ♍	1 ♉	1 12 ♍ ♎	1 ♊	1 ♎	1 ♋	1 20 ♎ ♏	1 25 ♋ ♌	1 ♏
OCT	1 ♒	1 ♎	1 30 ♉ ♈	1 ♎ ♏	1 17 ♊ ♋	1 ♎	1 27 ♋ ♌	1 ♏	1 ♌	1 7 ♏ ♐
NOV	1 6 ♒ ♓	1 15 ♎ ♏	1 ♈	1 ♏	1 26 ♋ ♊	1 21 ♏ ♐	1 ♌	1 2 ♏ ♐	1 20 ♌ ♍	1 22 ♐ ♒
DEC	1 26 ♓ ♈	1 30 ♏ ♐	1 24 ♈ ♉	1 11 ♏ ♐	1 ♊	1 ♐	1 ♌	1 13 ♐ ♑	1 ♍	1 31 ♑ ♒

– MARS TABLES –

♂	1981	1982	1983	1984	1985	1986	1987	1988	1989	1990
JAN	1 ♒	1 ♎	1 ♒ 17 ♓	1 ♎ 11 ♏	1 ♓	1 ♏	1 ♓ 8 ♈	1 ♏ 9 ♐	1 ♈ 19 ♉	1 ♐ 30 ♑
FEB	1 ♒ 7 ♓	1 ♎	1 ♓ 25 ♈	1 ♏	1 ♓ 3 ♈	1 ♏ 2 ♐	1 ♈ 21 ♉	1 ♐ 22 ♑	1 ♉	1 ♑
MAR	1 ♓ 17 ♈	1 ♎	1 ♈	1 ♏	1 ♈ 15 ♉	1 ♐ 28 ♑	1 ♉	1 ♑	1 ♉ 11 ♊	1 ♑ 12 ♒
APR	1 ♈ 25 ♉	1 ♎	1 ♈ 5 ♉	1 ♏	1 ♉ 26 ♊	1 ♑	1 ♉ 6 ♊	1 ♑ 7 ♒	1 ♊ 29 ♋	1 ♒ 21 ♓
MAY	1 ♉	1 ♎	1 ♉ 17 ♊	1 ♏	1 ♊	1 ♑	1 ♊ 21 ♋	1 ♒ 22 ♓	1 ♋	1 ♓ 31 ♈
JUN	1 ♉ 5 ♊	1 ♎	1 ♊ 29 ♋	1 ♏	1 ♊ 9 ♋	1 ♑	1 ♋	1 ♓	1 ♋ 17 ♌	1 ♈
JUL	1 ♊ 18 ♋	1 ♎	1 ♋	1 ♏	1 ♋ 25 ♌	1 ♑	1 ♋ 7 ♌	1 ♓ 14 ♈	1 ♌	1 ♈ 13 ♉
AUG	1 ♋	1 ♎ 3 ♏	1 ♋ 14 ♌	1 ♏ 18 ♐	1 ♌	1 ♑	1 ♌ 23 ♍	1 ♈	1 ♌ 3 ♍	1 ♉ 31 ♊
SEP	1 ♋ 2 ♌	1 ♏ 20 ♐	1 ♌ 30 ♍	1 ♐	1 ♌ 10 ♍	1 ♑	1 ♍	1 ♈	1 ♍ 20 ♎	1 ♊
OCT	1 ♌ 21 ♍	1 ♐	1 ♍	1 ♐ 5 ♑	1 ♍ 28 ♎	1 ♑ 9 ♒	1 ♍ 8 ♎	1 ♈ 24 ♓	1 ♎	1 ♊
NOV	1 ♍	1 ♑	1 ♍ 18 ♎	1 ♑ 16 ♒	1 ♎	1 ♒ 26 ♓	1 ♎ 24 ♏	1 ♓ 2 ♈	1 ♎ 4 ♏	1 ♊
DEC	1 ♍ 16 ♎	1 ♑ 10 ♒	1 ♎	1 ♒ 25 ♓	1 ♎ 15 ♏	1 ♓	1 ♏	1 ♈	1 ♏ 18 ♐	1 ♊ 14 ♉

♂	1991	1992	1993	1994	1995	1996	1997	1998	1999	2000
JAN	1 ♉ 21 ♊	1 ♐ 9 ♑	1 ♋	1 ♑ 28 ♒	1 ♍ 23 ♌	1 ♑ 9 ♒	1 ♍ 3 ♎	1 ♒ 25 ♓	1 ♎ 26 ♏	1 ♒ 4 ♓
FEB	1 ♊	1 ♑ 18 ♒	1 ♋	1 ♒	1 ♌	1 ♒ 15 ♓	1 ♎	1 ♓	1 ♏	1 ♓ 12 ♈
MAR	1 ♊	1 ♒ 28 ♓	1 ♋	1 ♒ 7 ♓	1 ♌	1 ♓ 25 ♈	1 ♎ 2 ♍	1 ♓ 5 ♈	1 ♏	1 ♈ 23 ♉
APR	1 ♊ 3 ♋	1 ♓	1 ♋ 28 ♌	1 ♓ 15 ♈	1 ♌	1 ♈	1 ♍	1 ♈ 13 ♉	1 ♏	1 ♉
MAY	1 ♋ 27 ♌	1 ♓ 6 ♈	1 ♌	1 ♈ 24 ♉	1 ♌ 26 ♍	1 ♈ 3 ♉	1 ♍	1 ♉ 24 ♊	1 ♏ 6 ♎	1 ♉ 4 ♊
JUN	1 ♌	1 ♈ 15 ♉	1 ♌ 23 ♍	1 ♉	1 ♍	1 ♉ 12 ♊	1 ♍ 19 ♎	1 ♊	1 ♎	1 ♊ 16 ♋
JUL	1 ♌ 16 ♍	1 ♉ 27 ♊	1 ♍	1 ♉ 4 ♊	1 ♍ 21 ♎	1 ♊ 26 ♋	1 ♎	1 ♊ 6 ♋	1 ♎ 5 ♏	1 ♋
AUG	1 ♍	1 ♊	1 ♍ 12 ♎	1 ♊ 17 ♋	1 ♎	1 ♋	1 ♎ 14 ♏	1 ♋ 21 ♌	1 ♏	1 ♌
SEP	1 ♎	1 ♊ 12 ♋	1 ♎ 27 ♏	1 ♋	1 ♎ 7 ♏	1 ♋ 10 ♌	1 ♏ 29 ♐	1 ♌	1 ♏ 3 ♐	1 ♌ 17 ♍
OCT	1 ♎ 17 ♏	1 ♋	1 ♏	1 ♋ 5 ♌	1 ♏ 21 ♐	1 ♌ 30 ♍	1 ♐	1 ♌ 2 ♍	1 ♐ 17 ♑	1 ♍
NOV	1 ♏ 29 ♐	1 ♋	1 ♏ 9 ♐	1 ♌	1 ♐	1 ♍	1 ♐ 9 ♑	1 ♍ 27 ♎	1 ♑ 26 ♒	1 ♍ 4 ♎
DEC	1 ♐	1 ♋	1 ♐ 20 ♑	1 ♌ 12 ♍	1 ♐	1 ♍	1 ♑ 18 ♒	1 ♎	1 ♒	1 ♎ 23 ♏